MY PET HAMSTER

BY NANCY GREENWOOD

Gareth Stevens
PUBLISHING

Please visit our website, www.garethstevens.com. For a free color catalog of all our high-quality books, call toll free 1-800-542-2595 or fax 1-877-542-2596.

Portions of this work were originally authored by Cecelia H. Brannon and published as *Pet Hamsters*. All new material this edition authored by Nancy Greenwood.

Library of Congress Cataloging-in-Publication Data
Names: Greenwood, Nancy, author.
Title: My pet hamster / Nancy Greenwood.
Description: New York : Gareth Stevens Publishing, [2023] | Series: My new pet | Includes index.
Identifiers: LCCN 2022000028 (print) | LCCN 2022000029 (ebook) | ISBN 9781538281048 (set) | ISBN 9781538281055 (library binding) | ISBN 9781538281031 (paperback) | ISBN 9781538281062 (ebook)
Subjects: LCSH: Hamsters as pets–Juvenile literature.
Classification: LCC SF459.H3 G74 2023 (print) | LCC SF459.H3 (ebook) | DDC 636.935/6–dc23/eng/20220111
LC record available at https://lccn.loc.gov/2022000028
LC ebook record available at https://lccn.loc.gov/2022000029

Published in 2023 by
Gareth Stevens Publishing
29 East 21st Street
New York, NY 10010

Copyright © 2023 Gareth Stevens Publishing

Designer: Andrea Davison-Bartolotta
Editor: Kristen Nelson

Photo credits: Cover, p. 1 marinakarpenko/Shutterstock.com; series art (interior backgrounds) Magnia/Shutterstock.com; p. 5 Andrew Angelov/Shutterstock.com; p. 7 (bottom left) Vinicius R. Souza/Shutterstock.com; p. 7 (bottom right) Mary Swift/Shutterstock.com; p. 7 (top left) ToNN Stocker/Shutterstock.com; p. 7 (top right) chaiyawat chaidet/Shutterstock.com; p. 9 Freer/Shutterstock.com; pp. 11, 17 stock_shot/Shutterstock.com; p. 13 Monika_1/Shutterstock.com; p. 15 WOLF 91/Shutterstock.com; p. 19 HelloRF Zcool/Shutterstock.com; p. 21 Karen H. Ilagan/Shutterstock.com.

Printed in the United States of America

Some of the images in this book illustrate individuals who are models. The depictions do not imply actual situations or events.

CPSIA compliance information: Batch #CSGS23: For further information contact Gareth Stevens, New York, New York at 1-800-542-2595.

Find us on

CONTENTS

Boldface words appear in the glossary.

Let's Get a Hamster!

Hamsters are often kept as pets. Like any pet, they need love and care. Are you ready for the **responsibility**? This book will help prepare you for life with your new friend, the hamster!

The Hamster Look

Hamsters are cute! They have small bodies with short legs and tails. They are covered in soft fur. It can be many colors. Hamsters are black, white, red, or brown. They can be a mix of colors too.

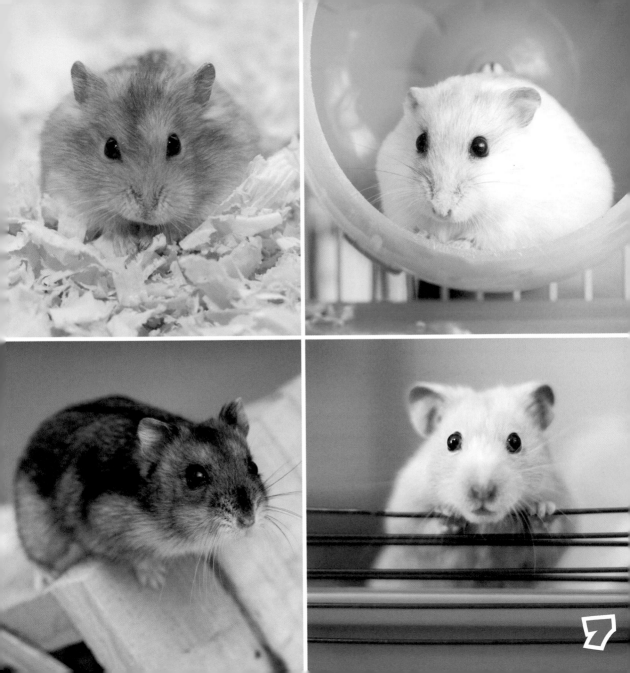

Hamster Life

Hamsters need a special cage to live in. It's important to be sure the cage is big enough for your hamster. The cage must be cleaned at least once a week. Hamsters are **nocturnal**. They may make noise at night while you sleep!

Staying Healthy

Pet hamsters eat seeds, nuts, and special food called **pellets**. But hamsters eat fruit too. You can share a healthy snack with your hamster! A hamster has special **pouches** in its cheeks. This is where it keeps food when it's not chewing it.

Like you, a pet hamster needs water to drink. A hamster drinks water from a special bottle in its cage. It needs fresh water every day. It can be your job to change the water! Fresh water keeps your hamster healthy.

Hamsters are **rodents**. Their teeth grow all the time. Hamsters need to chew to keep their teeth clean, sharp, and short. You can give a pet hamster special treats to chew, or some household items like paper towel tubes.

Hamsters are **popular** pets because they are easy to care for. You do not have to bathe a hamster. It will clean itself by wiping its fur with its paws. At least once a year, hamsters need to be taken to a **vet**.

Making Friends

Some hamsters like to live alone. Others, like dwarf hamsters, might like to live and play with a friend! Find out whether your type of hamster would like to **socialize** before adding another hamster pet to their cage.

18

You can play with your hamster too! Many hamsters like to be held. But, a pet hamster may bite if you bother it when it's sleeping! Take time to learn about your hamster's **personality**. You'll find the best way to play together!

GLOSSARY

nocturnal: Active at night.

pellet: A small, hard ball of food.

personality: A set of qualities or ways of acting that make a person or animal different from others.

popular: Liked by many people.

pouch: A pocket of skin inside the mouths of some animals.

responsibility: Something a person is in charge of.

rodent: A small, furry animal with large front teeth, such as a mouse or rat.

socialize: To do things with others in a friendly way.

vet: A doctor who is trained to treat animals. Vet is short for veterinarian.

FOR MORE INFORMATION

BOOKS

Osborne, M. K. *Curious About Hamsters*. Mankato, MN: Amicus, 2021.

Salzmann, Mary Elizabeth. *Hamsters Are Fun!* Minneapolis, MN: Sandcastle, an imprint of Abdo Publishing, 2022.

WEBSITES

Hamsters: From the Wild to Your Bedroom
kids.nationalgeographic.com/nature/article/wild-hamsters
Check out more information about hamsters here.

Pet Care for Kids
spca.bc.ca/programs-services/for-kids-teens/for-kids/pet-care-for-kids/
Read about different kinds of pets to see which one is right for you.

INDEX

leveled reader
science

MY NEW PET

MY NEW PET

MY PET
CAT

leveled reader

MY NEW PET

MY PET
DOG

leveled reader

MY NEW PET

MY PET
GOLDFISH

leveled reader

MY NEW PET

MY PET
HAMSTER

leveled reader

MY NEW PET

MY PET
PARAKEET

leveled reader

MY NEW PET

MY PET
RABBIT

leveled reader

ISBN: 9781538281031
6-pack ISBN: 9781538281048

9 781538 281031

Gareth Stevens
PUBLISHING